MW01672814

Endorsements

"As a former prison warden, I can attest to the devastating effects incarceration has on families. Although there is no way to tell just what effect prison will have on the inmate and his or her family, there is one certainty: difficulties will come. ***This booklet is a guidebook which provides practical insights for families attempting to navigate the system through uncharted waters.*** *Lennie's message is one of hope to those who now have prison as part of their daily lives."*

—***Jack Cowley****, national director,*
Alpha USA Prisons & Re-Entry

"Lennie's personal experience is invaluable in helping the reader understand the issues and emotions of the inmate as well as the family members. ***Each page is filled with wisdom, understanding, compassion and caring.*** *Every person who is touched by incarceration would benefit from reading this excellent resource!"*

—***Ann Edenfield Sweet****, executive director*
and founder, Wings Ministry

Sentenced —Now What?:

Relationships During Incarceration

Lennie Spitale

emis
Evangelism and Missions Information Service

Billy Graham Center
Wheaton College

Sentenced—Now What?:
Relationships During Incarceration
Lennie Spitale

Copyright © 2007. Published by Evangelism and Missions Information Service (EMIS), a division of the Billy Graham Center at Wheaton College.

EMIS
P.O. Box 794
Wheaton, IL 60189
Phone: 630.752.7158
Email: emis@wheaton.edu
Website: www.billygrahamcenter.org/emis

ISBN 978-1-879089-42-6

The IPM Library

Over two million people are incarcerated in the United States today. However, countless others are also affected: families, friends, children, correctional officers and victims, to name a few. Because of this, the Institute for Prison Ministries (IPM) at the Billy Graham Center at Wheaton College began the "IPM Library." The IPM Library seeks to share the gospel, increase the knowledge of those serving in correctional ministries and offer helpful information to offenders and their families, correctional officers and victims. There are several audience-specific series within the IPM Library. Each booklet within each series will include a situation-appropriate, evangelistic message.

This Series

Sentenced—Now What?: Relationships During Incarceration is the second booklet in the IPM Library Series for Families. The first booklet, *"Help! My Loved One Is in Jail. What Do I Do Now?"* was released in June 2007. The Family Series is designed to help families cope with the practical and relational aspects of having a loved one in jail.

About the Institute for Prison Ministries

The Institute for Prison Ministries (IPM) is a department of the Billy Graham Center at Wheaton

College in Wheaton, Illinois. IPM is a networking, training and resource center for those who share the gospel within the correctional world. For more information, log on to: www.bgcprisonministries.com.

Acknowledgements

To my wife, Gwen, whose love for the Lord and desire to serve him is a constant encouragement to me. Her faith in our great God continues to grow and is demonstrated by a determination to shed worldly pursuits and to fill her thoughts and purposes for his kingdom.

To Karen Swanson, director of the Institute for Prison Ministries at the Billy Graham Center at Wheaton College, whose partnership and collaboration have been a great motivation.

To prison ministry people, whose tireless efforts to bring Christ's compassion behind bars are a testimony to God's faithfulness.

To the prisoners and their families, who suffer separation and personal pain, and are the very people for whom this has been written. May each of you find the true comfort that is found only in Jesus Christ and through faith in him.

To God, the source of all comfort, "who comforts us in all our troubles so that we can comfort others with the same comfort we ourselves have received from him" (2 Corinthians 1:3-4).

Contents

Introduction

Every ear in the courtroom strains to hear what will happen next. The judge is about to pronounce his or her sentence on your loved one. Like the pause between lightning and thunder, it seems like a tiny slice of eternity passes before the judge's words fill the air. And then it thunders. Your loved one is starting a prison sentence. The long uncertainty of the arrest and trial period is over. Now what?

This second booklet in the Institute for Prison Ministries Library series is designed to help you with this next phase of the incarceration journey. Unlike the first booklet (*"Help! My Loved One Is in Jail. What Do I Do Now?"*), which spoke to legal issues you were facing, this booklet will not address any continued legal steps (such as appeals, motions and various hearings) you may be taking. Instead, it will act as a roadmap to answer questions such as: Where will your loved one go? What should you expect to happen next? How do we communicate? Most importantly, however, this booklet will help to protect and build your relationship with your loved one while steel bars separate the two of you.

CHAPTER ONE

Where to Start

Unless your loved one was allowed the rare privilege of reporting to prison at a later date than the sentencing, you have already experienced the unforgettable visual image of watching him[1] led out of the courtroom in handcuffs and away to prison. Perhaps you were allowed a brief kiss or hug, or your lawyer managed to arrange a few words in private. However, a whole new chapter is about to begin. You quickly promise each other you will write and visit, but neither of you knows how the details will unfold. A new set of fears emerge. Your final, fleeting moments have a dreamlike quality to them, and somewhere in the back of both your minds is a voice asking, "What will life be like now?"

Culture Shock

Going to prison is like being buried alive. You are neither dead nor free. It's like walking through a bad dream; and like one who dreams, it almost seems like you are watching the events unfold from

1. As in the first booklet, for simplicity we continue to use the pronoun "he" for the incarcerated individual. We do this with the full understanding that those arrested can be either male or female.

some other place. You know it is happening, but it's as though part of your mind has not caught up with reality.

When new inmates are processed through the unfamiliar territory of the facility for the first time, they are starkly aware that the steel doors are sliding shut on more than just physical space; they are declaring an end to life as they have known it. Everything has changed. Everything is changing. And yet, in the days ahead everything will become monotonously the same.

Individuality, and all those appearances on the outside that make us different from other people, are systematically stripped away. Little things, like surrendering street clothes for the sameness of state-issued colors, are like foreign road signs announcing one's arrival to this dark country. Economic differences, social differences, even our personal tastes and preferences, become reduced to the level playing field of the prison. The world we thought only briefly about as we passed a correctional facility in our cars, or watched on television, has become a reality we never thought we would have to face. The nightmare has begun.[2]

Time and Place

While every day in jail is a day too long, the journey is quite different for those facing several years or more. The "shorter" inmates (a term given to

---

2. For a more detailed account of what life is like from the prisoner's perspective, see Spitale, Lennie. 2002. *Prison Ministry: Understanding Prison Culture Inside and Out*. Nashville, Tenn.: Broadman & Holman Publishers.

someone whose sentence is fairly close to completion) tend to think in terms of life as a giant "pause button." They are concerned with pacing themselves to get to the finish line. Those facing several years of actual incarceration must come to grips with the fact that prison is going to be their home for a while. To constantly think about the exit gate will only make their time more difficult. And while it is true that all inmates think about going home, those with lengthier sentences must now think about how they will settle into this life for the immediate future. For the sake of clearer communication, this booklet refers to the short-timer as a "county" inmate and the long-timer as a "state" inmate.

County Sentences vs. State Sentences

County jail sentences are usually less than 2 1/2 years in duration. And while the exact limit that qualifies for a "county sentence" may vary from region to region, most will fall between 1 to 2 1/2 years. State sentences can range from one or two years to life without parole. In the federal system, the length of incarceration can be short or long. Since the crime committed was a federal offense, the convicted person does not qualify for either a state or a county sentence. And although there are federal inmates serving time in state facilities, these are usually due to protection issues or other special security concerns.

No Two Alike

While many prisons look alike, every correctional facility is a little empire unto itself, and is governed as such. Institutions may appear similar in terms of security classifications, essential rules, correctional structure and whether or not they are state, county or federal, but that is where the similarities end. Every jail or prison is different in terms of:

- its correctional environment
- the mindset of its staff
- the age of the institution
- the philosophy of the administration
- the regional culture
- the type of inmates housed
- differing protocols, rules and regulations
- the variety (or lack) of its programs
- the ratio of volunteers, counselors or caseworkers
- meeting space
- availability of religious expressions

One additional factor is the availability of programs, which can affect the overall morale of the inmates. Generally speaking, many programs = better morale. Few programs = grumbling and complaints. The combination of these elements, and others, combine to affect the inmate's overall experience. Every prison has its own unique history, lore and personality; your loved one will soon become familiar with them.

Questions surrounding visitation also have a bearing on how the current struggle feels—and it affects those on both sides of the wall.

- How far away is the prison?
- Does the institution have contact visits or must visitors speak through a phone or glass partition?
- How much time is allotted for the visit?

- Are food items available in the visiting room?
- Are there places for children to play?
- Are the visiting times convenient?
- How long are the lines?
- How private are the conversations?
- How polite is the staff during the entry process?

Some prisons and jails are run very tightly; lock downs and shakedowns are common and prisoners feel oppressed. Others are run very loosely; contraband, drugs and weapons abound and everyone feels unsafe. Some are run professionally; others seem less so.

The collective mindset of the correctional staff is also a factor. Are they courteous and professional, or do they seem cold and intimidating? Numerous other factors contribute to an institution's unique personality, but the main point to remember is that every facility is different.

This could be important to you in terms of keeping a right perspective because you may have followed your loved one from (or have had exposure to) another correctional facility. If you or your loved one is expecting a similar experience, be prepared for a surprise. It may be a pleasant surprise (better conditions than the last facility), or it may be unpleasant (worse conditions). You must both adjust your expectations to rise or fall based on your new reality. If you attempt to log a complaint based on a comparison with another jurisdiction or facility, you will not likely get anything changed and it will only serve to add to your frustrations.

County Jail Sentences (shorter time)

If your loved one received a county sentence, it is likely he will be doing time in the very facility in which he sat while awaiting trial. If this happens, the adjustment each of you must make in terms of procedures and rules will be much easier. You may experience some changes in visiting schedules and procedures, but things will continue much as before. The greatest difference your loved one will experience is probably a change of location within the jail itself. By law, most states are required to keep "sentenced" inmates separate from "un-sentenced" inmates. While there are some security reasons for this (such as separation from enemies or co-defendants), the main reason is a constitutional one. Placing non-sentenced inmates with those who have already been convicted of a crime is a violation of the "innocent-until-proven-guilty" principle. For this reason, the courts have supported the notion that individuals cannot be *presumed* guilty by placing them with those who have already been *proven* guilty.[3] However, once found guilty, this constitutional wall disappears and your loved one will be placed in the "General Population" (also known as "GP" or "pop"), along with other convicted inmates.

What it potentially means for you is that his visiting times will probably change. In some jails, you may actually have *more* time allotted for visits than you previously had. It also means that his privileges and opportunities for self-help programs may also

---

3. Due to overcrowding, this principle is occasionally (but increasingly) violated.

improve. County facilities do not generally provide many programmatic or vocational opportunities for inmates in a pre-trial status; they would rather use the money on those who have been officially sentenced to their care. Your loved one may also be eligible for a working assignment, thus making his time a little easier by occupying his mind with something other than his own thoughts. Although paying jobs are more common in state facilities, some counties provide minimal pay that enables residents to purchase extra goodies from the canteen. Some residents even manage to send money home.

You should strongly encourage your loved one to take advantage of any program for which he is eligible to participate. First, it takes better advantage of the time. Second, the documentation of completed programs may help when it comes time to be considered for probation or parole.

Once sentenced, your loved one's security classification may immediately change. For example, he may go from a "maximum" security level to a "medium" or even a "minimum" level. This will have a direct impact on his privileges and can also improve your visiting status and environment. In some cases, your loved one may qualify for a "work release" status, permitting him to work outside the institution in the local community. While this minimum security level is not usually permitted until the inmate is close to the end of his sentence, the very fact that it could be available at some point serves as an encouraging milestone in his journey.

Time spent incarcerated while awaiting trial counts as time served on the sentence. If the sentence was not lengthy, he may already be eligible for work release. When I was in prison years ago, time served while awaiting trial did not count. It was simply lost time. This is no longer the situation in most states today.

The greatest advantage of a county sentence is that you have a targeted goal—you know the release date. During your loved one's awaiting-trial period, the future seemed so uncertain. Now, at least, you know what you are dealing with.

State Prison Sentences (longer time)

If your loved one has received a state sentence (more than two years), you, too, know what you are dealing with in terms of a release date. However, in your case, it seems like the reunion is so very far away. In the first year of incarceration, it is not uncommon for a new inmate to be transferred to one or two different institutions before he is finally sent to the facility where he will spend the greatest portion of his sentence.

The reasons for this are twofold. First, most states have what they call "classification facilities."[4] That is, correctional facilities that are used primarily to "classify" the most appropriate prison location for your loved one. Factors such as: type of crime committed, personality issues, prior convictions, problems with certain inmates, gang affiliations and medical conditions are all considered. Do not be overly concerned if you do not hear from your loved one for a week or so immediately

---

4. Sometimes called "Receiving" or "Reception & Diagnostic" (R&D prisons)

after sentencing. This is normal. The classification period often prevents immediate communication with the family. He will attempt to phone you as soon as he is permitted.

Second, some states have "disciplinary" prisons through which a new inmate may initially have to pass. These are typically maximum security facilities that house inmates who are getting into trouble within the correctional system. However, in some states, it is standard procedure for any newly sentenced person to arrive here for an indeterminate amount of time as part of the normal classification

Do not be overly concerned if you do not hear from your loved one for a week or so immediately after sentencing.

process. It is also, to a lesser degree, a chance for the Department of Corrections (DOC) to observe him. If he demonstrates he is going to be compliant, he will more than likely be moved to a more moderate facility shortly after the initial observation period is over. Additionally, the security department may feel that by immediately exposing him to the harder environment of a high security prison, the experience may serve as a deterrent to bad behavior. Residents in maximum security prisons have fewer programs and much less time out of their cells than do inmates in medium security prisons. Mentally, sentences served in these maximum facilities are what inmates refer to as "doing hard time."

If this initial hop-scotching journey appears to be your state's normal procedure for new inmates, do not be overly alarmed that your loved one has been sent to such a high security place. If he demonstrates that he will not be a problem, he will be moved to another facility after a few months, or even weeks. (Exceptions to this would be if the crime committed was of an unusually serious nature or has received a lot of media attention. In such cases, he may be there longer.)

New Learning Curve

Often, the variety of foreign experiences surrounding a loved one's early movements upon entering the prison system is unnerving to family members. It is normal to experience feelings of fear and inadequacy in terms of adjusting to this intimidating social setting. But try to keep in mind that over time you will become increasingly familiar with the way the system operates and your initial fears will diminish. Countless others have had to make the same adjustments; you are not alone in your struggle.

Once your loved one has finally arrived at the facility in which he will be doing the largest portion of his time, you will begin to adjust to the routine, rules and personalities you will meet. Prisons are all about routine; the very nature of the place requires it. But routine is your friend and will aid in your adjustment.

Finally, the best advice your loved one can receive when entering prison for the first time is to keep a low profile. The less attention he attracts to himself, the better.

CHAPTER TWO

Relationship Maintenance

A disruption the size of a tidal wave has taken place in the flow of your relationship; a major response will be required. You must determine to be proactive in how you are going to face this challenge. If you each make a commitment to not let this experience dictate the direction of your relationship, you will have a far better chance of staying above the floodwaters. When it comes to maintaining a healthy relationship with a loved one in prison, "offense is the best defense." It is not a time to be passive. Give careful thought about how you will nurture this relationship throughout the days and years ahead.

In my book, *Prison Ministry: Understanding Prison Culture Inside and Out*, I wrote:

> As most individuals who are caught for a crime they have committed experience, life on the outside is usually interrupted very suddenly. It doesn't matter that you have been sharing your life with people whom you love. It doesn't matter that you were in the middle of a mutual routine. Suddenly, you are cut off from them. And, as far as the pain itself goes, it doesn't even matter that you have brought it upon yourself or that the lifestyle you were leading made such a trip almost inevitable; it is still there. Not only for yourself, but also for those you

have left behind. If it is a girlfriend, the pain of sudden, complete separation comes crashing in on you. If it is a wife who has been good to you, it is even worse. If there are young children, it is worse still. The greatest pain of incarceration is the forcible separation from those you hold most dear.[5]

The book recorded the estimation that nearly eighty percent of married individuals are divorced within the first year of incarceration. Whether or not that percentage stills holds, one thing is abundantly clear: this experience is going to put a tremendous strain on any relationship, especially those of husbands and wives. While loss of freedom is one side of incarceration's double-edged sword of pain, forced separation from loved ones is the other.

Healthy Communication: The Key to Survival

The single most important aspect of maintaining any healthy relationship is effective communication. If this is true of society in general, it becomes absolutely essential in prison where the "big three" of communications are telephone calls, letters and visits. Each one has its own unique advantages and disadvantages. In the outside world, we take communication for granted. Face-to-face conversations, shared lifestyles and a wave of new technologies keep us in constant contact with each other. The limitations of prison communication cause us to be more appreciative (and thankful)

---

5. Spitale. 2002, 6.

for the means of communication that we do have. In fact, our moments of contact now become more precious than ever. We are far less likely to take our conversations for granted and far more likely to use the time wisely.

Because your future relationship depends so much upon phone calls, letters and visits, we will now examine how each one can play an important role in your relationship.

1. Telephone calls. Hearing a loved one's voice while in prison is like a lifeline to sanity. It is conversation—in real time—with that special someone. Only a face-to-face visit beats a phone call in terms of intimacy. However, there are two factors that must be considered up front: deciding how often to talk and deciding which times to call.

a. Deciding how often to talk. Phone calls from prison are expensive. And no matter how the prison has set up its particular phone system, payment always falls upon those on the outside.[6] At first, the one serving time is not always sensitive to this financial burden. Rational considerations such as thinking through how the phone bills will be paid tend to get shoved down in terms of priority. The frequency (or infrequency) of accepting calls from prisons and jails have been the fuel of many embittered and angry discussions. For the sake of your relationship, it is essential you come to a mutual agreement early in your new experience.

If your loved one formerly sat in the county jail before sentencing, you have probably already dealt

---

6. Unfortunately, it is not uncommon for phone bills to exceed several hundred dollars each month.

with the price of phone calls by the time he has reached the state system. Now the only question is a matter of frequency. How often is it financially feasible to speak to each other by phone? This discussion should be one of the first topics to be ironed out if the relationship is to continue to build in a positive way. Be sensitive to each other's needs. For those on the outside, realize how desperately your loved one wants to hear your voice. For those on the inside, be aware and concerned about your loved one's mounting financial pressures.

Here again, routine can become your friend. State inmates facing significant time tend to adjust more quickly to what is; county inmates have a more difficult time understanding why outside people cannot accept their phone calls more often. Come to an acceptable compromise as soon as possible—and stick to it. If finances or other factors change for the better, you can always renegotiate the topic at a later time. It is also important to have this discussion regarding phone frequency when both of you are in the right frame of mind. If you do not, one of you may agree to something you will later regret.

b. Deciding which times to call. Once you have decided on how often it is reasonable to call, the next step is to agree upon which times one can expect the calls to be made. Establishing a routine increases the likelihood that the person on the outside will be home when the call is made. If a relationship between a husband and wife (or boyfriend and girlfriend) is currently on shaky ground, insecure inmates tend to become overly worried (and imaginative) when they repeatedly get the answering machine.

There are several other factors to consider when preparing for phone conversations with your loved one.

1. Do not expect phone calls to be long and relaxed. Your loved one can only call during certain established times and he is not the only inmate who wants to use the phone.

2. Do not be distressed by sounds you hear in the background. Most phones are in the living units so it is normal to hear yelling and intercom announcements in the background. You may even overhear profanity or angry exchanges. While this can be initially distressing, be assured that your loved one has already begun to tune the noise out. Most residents try to respect the privacy of others when they are in the vicinity of the phones, but the living areas inside jails and prisons are not known for their acoustic sensitivity.

3. Remember that your conversations may be monitored. Although most administrations do not have the time, staff or inclination to eavesdrop on every phone conversation, they can (and occasionally do) record what you say.

4. For holidays, consider calling a few days prior to (or after) the event. Not only is the volume of traffic for telephone companies high on holidays, but the few available telephones at the prison are also in high demand. Tempers can be short if inmates appear to be hogging the phones. If you do call before or after the special day, make sure to arrange this ahead of time so that no one will be disappointed.

5. Cell phone issues. Obviously, inmates cannot have cell phones. Their popularity has created such a major security concern for the correctional industry that they now rank right alongside drugs and weapons on any list of serious contraband items. For inmates to have uncensored telephone access to the outside world is a justifiable concern for security officials. And, since phone technology now includes access to the Internet, it becomes even more worrisome. Many telephone systems within correctional facilities do not even allow calls to a cell phone, thereby creating an additional problem for those families who have only a wireless service as their primary line.

Advantages of using the phone. The advantage of using the phone lies in its real-time access to your loved one. There is nothing like hearing the comfort of an "I love you" in the midst of this dark storm. It is also immediate communication during times of pressing family problems. If little Johnny is having problems at school, dad can speak to him directly and provide counsel or comfort. If a couple's relationship is on shaky ground, things can be hashed out in real time. If other pressing family problems exist, suggestions for resources or assistance can also be made.

Disadvantages of using the phone. The downsides of a phone call are usually created when disagreements occur. If a difference of opinion escalates into a full-blown argument, the call usually ends badly. Remember, due to limited phone time you may not be able to "make up" before the communication ends. If either of you feels the call is heading in a negative direction, try to delay the subject for another time. If you sense an argument heating up, offer to explain your side of the issue in your next letter. While the communication may still end on a down note, you will have prevented it from getting worse.

The chaplain's phone for emergencies only. In emergencies, such as the hospitalization or death of a family member, most facilities allow inmates to use the chaplain's phone. However, for the sake of gaining access to this privilege when it is really needed, encourage your loved one to seek it only in these specific instances. The high price of phone calls, combined with the quiet privacy of the chaplain's office, makes the chaplain's phone a great temptation for inmates. Most chaplains will tell you that they are constantly fending off requests for the use of their phone. And while one can hardly blame the inmates for trying, the chaplain is more apt to allow its use to someone who seldom bothers him or her for it. In the case of those extreme family emergencies, most chaplains are happy to provide this resource, but he or she will have to verify the message with the appropriate sources before granting permission.

The chaplain is one of the inmate's most important resources in terms of providing encouragement, advice and spiritual comfort. If the need should ever arise, consider speaking to the chaplain yourself if you feel your loved one could use his or her services. A chaplain can drop by your loved one's cell at almost any time, just to see how he is doing.

2. Letters. Mail call is the highlight of the day for most prisoners. The mood of an entire 24-hour period can rest upon whether or not a letter from a loved one was received. I have watched how tenderly a stack of envelopes can be taken out of their special places and referred to as "lifelines" by someone in prison. Those of us on the outside can sometimes fail to realize how important a letter is to a dear soul living his life out in this lonely place. I have been guilty of forgetting this myself. There have been occasions when I have allowed months

I have watched how tenderly a stack of envelopes can be taken out of their special places and referred to as "life-lines" by someone in prison.

to go by before responding to a friend in prison. And although they are always very forgiving, I know I have disappointed them.

It is all too easy to let one day slip into another. "I'll write tomorrow," we say to ourselves. Then tomorrow becomes next week, and before we know it, a month has gone by. This procrastination can be devastating to your incarcerated loved one who is beginning to imagine all sorts of fears as to why you have not written. But remember: letters don't always have to be long. Most inmates would rather have two or three short letters in a month than one long epistle every other month.

Spouses who are deeply in love, as well as starstruck boyfriends and girlfriends, write each other frequently. Some try to write every day. But even in these cases, the demands and responsibilities of outside life can cause an occasional delay. The person in prison does everything (including writing letters) at pretty much the same time every day; it, too, has become a part of his fixed routine. As a result, if there is a sudden drop in the frequency of letters coming in from the outside, it is immediately noticed by the one inside. In such instances (and there will be such instances), the loved one behind the walls must keep in mind that life on the outside is much more demanding in terms of responsibilities.

For those who have already been in prison for years, the flow of letters is no longer at the volume that it once was. Even between married couples, a new routine has become the acceptable pattern. As long as the frequency of letters is mutually agreed upon, it is less likely to be perceived as a decline in commitment. As with phone calls, if you can come to an agreement early as to how often one can reasonably expect to receive mail, it will help to keep imaginations in check.

Advantages of letter writing. Do not underestimate the power of the letter. It has several strong advantages over phone calls and visits. The first is that it provides insight into your heart and thoughts without fear of interruption. Your loved one will read your letter to the end (and often several times over). It doesn't matter whether or not you think you write well; it's you your loved one wants to hear from.

Another great advantage of composing a letter is that you can reread it before you send it. Did you say what you wanted to say? How will it sound to the recipient? If you wrote in a fit of anger or frustration, you can set it aside for a while before sending it. My suggestion is not to seal it right away. Set it aside until enough time has passed for you to allow your emotions to settle down. You may be surprised to discover that what you wrote originally is not exactly the way you feel now.

Letters also have a way of expressing our deepest thoughts. The slower pace of writing enables us to express ourselves more carefully. Your heart is communicating its passion in words, without the interruption of physical affection. And while the physical affection may be far more desirable to each of you, love grows as we share the intimacy of our inner thoughts.

Although receiving a letter is viewed as a bit less satisfying than visits or phone calls, its strategic importance should not be underestimated when it comes to maintaining a healthy relationship. Do not dismiss it as less important than the other forms of communication. While the other two forms have a greater sense of immediate gratification, revealing one's heart through letters is a major building block in any relationship.

Regulations regarding letters. As with everything else in the DOC, there are rules about writing letters. Find out what your loved one's institution will and will not permit. You can usually get this information from your loved one, who is given an inmate "rule book" that includes various regulations. This will include mail procedures. However, if you do not have access to this information yet, below are some general procedures that may be helpful.

1. *Addressing envelopes.* Most correctional facilities are very particular about how you address your envelopes. Many require that the inmate's institutional number be added after his name. (If you do not know this number, ask your loved one for it the next time he communicates with you.) Many facilities will return your letter to you if this ID number is not included. Some state DOC websites have inmate searches where you can find the inmate identification number, as well as a list of prohibited items and how to send money.

2. *Items included in letter.* Prisons and jails have regulations regarding what items you are allowed to place inside a letter. A few will allow you to enclose postage stamps; but increasingly, most will not. You cannot enclose letters or notes from anyone else but yourself. If you are unsure about what is permitted, a good rule of thumb is to not enclose anything but the actual letter. However, if you do enclose an article you thought seemed innocent, usually the worst that will happen is your item will be returned to you. (Sometimes accompanied by a short, stamped explanation.)

3. *Enclosing money/money orders.* You cannot send cash. However, in most cases, you may enclose a money order (not a personal check) if you wish to contribute to your loved one's canteen fund or commissary (inmate account). If this is the procedure allowed, write his inmate ID number after his name on the "pay to" line of the money order. Do

not make it out to the institution. If you are sending it along with personal correspondence, write in the body of the letter that you have enclosed the money order and for how much. In the event that the check should ever become separated from the letter, or if the institution delays too long in getting the money order to the resident for signing, your loved one at least knows you have sent the money.

4. *Enclosing pictures.* Pictures are usually allowed as long as they are not inappropriate or sexually suggestive. Avoid sending large photos, or too many at one time. Short clippings from a hometown newspaper are usually allowed as well. However, only a commercial bookstore or publisher can generally send published literature, such as books or magazines. In such cases, place the order with the bookstore and have it sent directly to the recipient. Find out what your institution requires about this if you plan on sending such items.

5. *Content of the letter.* The content of a letter can also be examined. All correspondence is subject to being read by prison officials prior to delivery to the inmate. Any portion of a paragraph or sentence can be censored or blacked out. This includes mail coming in, as well as mail going out. Some institutions prohibit letters that are too graphic in terms of sexual content or contain references to transportation dates or other inmates.

6. *Receiving a letter from prison.* Be prepared to find that letters showing up in your mailbox may be clearly identified as coming from a correctional facility. Some institutions go so far as to stamp in bright blue or red ink: "This letter has been sent

from a correctional facility" (or some such similar identification) on the envelope.

7. *Illegal items.* Do not attempt to send anything illegal. Depending upon the item, this could result in criminal charges being brought against you. At minimum, you will lose visiting privileges and it may also result in disciplinary action against your loved one.

Pen pal ministries. Pen pal correspondence generally refers to letters that did not develop from a previous relationship with the inmate. The name of the resident was acquired by some secondary means, and a pen pal friendship began. This friendship can be a very rewarding and encouraging experience for both parties, and can make many difficult hours pass more pleasantly for inmates. However, there are still some serious cautions that need to be understood before starting this form of communication. Insincere motives and manipulation are not uncommon. In light of the intimacy that can quickly develop through letters, it is strongly urged that you start this activity under the guidance of a credible letter-writing program or ministry. Do not respond to an ad in the paper or on the Internet, or write "the friend of a friend."[7]

3. Visits. By far, the most enjoyable of the three forms of communication is the face-to-face visit; it is one of the most anticipated moments in the incarceration journey. Visiting day is usually the second most-circled date on an inmate's calendar. (Only parole hearings or the day of release have

7. For a more complete list of cautions and recommendations, go to www.bgcprisonministries.com. Once there, go to: chaplains, ministry workers & volunteers / materials / pen pals. Then click on "guidelines for letter writing."

greater significance.) Yet for all its anticipated arrival, the experience itself is often bittersweet. Visits bring us tantalizingly close to the very people we care most about in this world; however, the inevitable good-bye is always lurking in the sounds of the clock on the wall.

But we know we cannot spend the whole time stressing about how soon the visit will end. Loved ones must now focus on a way to enjoy the moments they have, and to utilize the time rekindling (and maintaining) their relationship. When considered in a more positive light, it is probably the only occasion that a prisoner can honestly say he wished the time didn't go so fast. That, in itself, is a rare blessing in prison!

Finding a unique visiting routine. Eventually, you will both settle into a visiting routine that is as unique as the two of you. There is no prescribed way in which you must occupy yourselves during your visit. One size does not fit all, and what works for one pair of visitors may not be suitable for another. I once observed a man and woman who immediately sat down, took out a deck of cards and chatted sporadically over a game of gin rummy for their entire visit. Throughout the years of his incarceration, they had carved out a unique routine that was as normal and comfortable for them as any married couple anywhere. It wasn't how I would particularly choose to spend my entire visit, but their ease of conversation and the apparent contentment of their hours spent together was enough to tell me that it worked well for them. You too, must find what works best for you. Just remember to give yourselves enough time to figure this out. Comfortable adjustment doesn't come quickly or easily.

The emotional side. As a side note, be aware that there are some individuals who find visits too emotionally difficult. Although most residents would not refuse a visit if someone showed up, there are some who would prefer to not put themselves or their loved ones through such an emotionally charged experience. For example, when I was in prison, I did not want many visits from the outside world. I didn't want to be so freshly reminded of all the things that I couldn't have. My world was the prison and I felt I needed to focus on those things I had to deal with inside its walls. For me, outside realities had to take a back seat. But I was also a short-timer by most prison standards and would probably have felt differently if I were serving a longer sentence. I mention this only because visits, as wonderful as they can be, have a painful side to them; there are those who, for whatever reason, choose not to have too many of them. If this is the case with your loved one, be sensitive to his request for fewer visits, but feel free to gently challenge that decision, especially if you feel your loved one is not adjusting well. Life is hard, and especially life in prison. Attempting to protect ourselves from painful emotions may seem understandable, but it doesn't help us grow socially. It especially doesn't help the growth of a relationship that seeks to do more than just survive.

Visits keep the relationship in a healthy balance, especially so if you are a husband and wife. In the Bible, God said, "It is not good for a man to be alone."[8] As painful or as logistically difficult as your visits might be, they are extremely helpful in your continued quest to build oneness in your marriage. A person who is tempted to withdraw from physical visits may eventually find himself withdrawing emotionally as well. You are among the few who know your loved one best; help him to overcome this hurdle.

The visitor's point of view. Visits also create challenges that are more difficult for the visitor than the one in prison. Loved ones serving time in correctional facilities need to demonstrate great sympathy and patience when it comes to the sacrifice their visitors must often make just to get there. It may seem unnecessary to state this, but experience has shown that many inmates are not always in tune with this sacrifice. The severe hardships of their own present reality have so overwhelmed them that they can often become self-absorbed.

The negative realities of prison life create a strong sense of survival in those who must live there. While this sense of survival is necessary, it can diminish their awareness of how much others are suffering. Visitors new to this environment can also feed into their loved one's preoccupation with self by feeling excessively sorry or afraid for them. But over time, if the visiting experience continues to be dominated by the self-focused circumstances of the resident, it does little to help him grow socially. If it continues, the visitors themselves may feel less motivated to keep coming.

---

8. Genesis 2:18

No Man's Land: The Visiting Room

Two different worlds are colliding in a neutral zone called the visiting room. For the prisoner, this special place is a safety zone within the prison that he is seldom permitted to enter. Since the only time he is allowed in there is when someone special to him is present, the room doesn't have the same negative feelings attached to it that he assigns to the other places of the prison. For him, it becomes a pleasant "no man's land" closer to the outside world. For the visitor, however, it is as close to the bowels of the prison as he or she cares to go.

And yet, through the magic of their mutual presence, the walls of this room, whatever the color, seem to brighten with a mixture of joy and togetherness. But as anticipated as the visiting experience is, a surprising number of them do not go well. "How can this be?" you ask. "How is it that such a joyous meeting could turn out to be anything less than a small piece of heaven?" The reasons have less to do with our good intentions, and more to do with our lack of cultural preparedness.

In reality, all relationships have difficulties; it is a part of growing together. But the heavy stress of the incarceration experience tends to inflate disagreements out of proportion. As a result, the prisoner can fear that he is slowly losing the object of his affection, and feels powerless to prevent it. Meanwhile, the visitor may sense that his or her loved one is withdrawing, or emotionally changing for the worse. A true perspective is desperately needed.

People on the outside seldom think about the multiple occasions in which they are involved in social settings with friends and family. They casually enjoy the simple pleasure of just being together. But sparse and precious moments in the visiting room carry the constant awareness of impending separation. Loved ones fight bravely to stuff the easy flow of a natural relationship into an unnatural amount of time. And when a difference of opinion arises, they can feel pressured to artificially "fix" the disagreement before the officer says visiting time is over. This creates a two-fold challenge for you and your loved one. First, conflicts take time to work out. Second, your ruffled emotions will have a difficult time catching up to the hands on the clock, even if the issue does get resolved.

Conflict is necessary in any relationship because no two people are the same—everyone has different opinions and perspectives. So conflict, in itself, is not a bad thing; it is a natural part of any growing relationship. In the casual ebb and flow of couples on the outside, conflicts can be more easily worked out because time is a friend. But when conflicts arise between loved ones experiencing a prison visit, the few moments of togetherness can feel greatly threatened. Both people are keenly aware that any difference of opinion can quickly escalate into a heated, unresolved argument by the time the bell rings to say goodbye. In an effort to avoid such an escalation, couples may try to stay away from topics that often need the most to be discussed. The sweet shortness of the prison visit tempts them to compress their intimacy into a few seconds, and to not talk about those things that could threaten it. But by doing so, they risk staying in the shallow waters of their relationship.

So how do we overcome this? One suggestion is that each person should become more aware of the combined effect of the three forms of communication. Remember, each form has a strength that the others do not. For example, when a difference of perspective creates a conflict, letters are perhaps the best tools for detailing how each of you feels. A written narrative, carefully explaining your perspective, will give you a chance to be heard without fear of interruption. The phone call, on the other hand, can be a quick referee. "A letter is coming," you might say, "promise me you'll read it carefully before you jump to conclusions."

All that is really different between you and any couple on the outside is that your methods of communication will have to be more creative.

Help each other realize the limitations of your visit and try hard to keep things in perspective. Remember, conflicts are normal and necessary in any relationship. All that is really different between you and any couple on the outside is that your methods of communication will have to be more creative.

The point to remember, however, is that the added stress of incarceration can cause even the best of visits to go unexpectedly sour. I once addressed this phenomenon in an article I wrote. Here is a portion of it:

Men and women in prison often express to me that they know how hard it is for their loved ones to visit them. Distances can be great and gas prices high. Some of their visitors have very little extra money and have to rely on public transportation or the kindness of friends to get there. Maybe they had to arrange for a babysitter or take time off work. Responsibilities had to be postponed in order to get to the prison. And then there is the whole, humiliating experience of the entry process! The lines and the lockers, the searches and the metal detectors. By the time they finally sit down, they feel like they've been caught up in an exhausting whirlwind of experiences. They know the inmate had only to wash up, comb his hair and bounce off to the visiting room when his name was called. But the prisoner lives in a crude and negative world and it's not always easy to shake it off when it comes time for the meeting.[9]

Following is a slight expansion of the ten suggestions with which I concluded the article referenced above. When you come together for your visit:

1. Verbally acknowledge that each other's stress is real. You are temporarily living in two different worlds. Let the other person know you are aware his or her battle is difficult. Empathize and comment, but do not pretend to fully understand the other's stress factors.

2. Give each other adequate time to express feelings. I usually recommend that the one in jail allows the visitor to be the one who talks about his or her life first. The prison world is a small one.

---

9. Spitale, Lennie. 2006. "Visiting Room Sabotage" in *Inside Journal*. 17(4): 1, 7. Used by permission. *Inside Journal* is a bimonthly, Christian newspaper read by inmates across the country. It is published by Prison Fellowship (www.pfm.org).

By listening to outside experiences first, it will help expand the variety of conversation.

3. Give each other the freedom to be honest. Trust is built by having a safe place to express one's honest emotions. One great advantage of the visiting experience is that it forces conversation by minimizing the more intense forms of physical communication. While most (especially lovers) would see this as a great disadvantage, it forces the other person to convey his or her inner feelings through words. (This is also the main reason why many relationships begin in prison.) But a note of caution is in order: if either person is experiencing deep feelings of distrust or jealousy, and is unable to successfully control them, it may be best to hold the discussion for another time. In such cases, the old saying, "If you can't handle the truth, don't ask for it," may be the better choice.

4. Remember that there is a time for everything. Agree together whether or not the timing is right to bring up certain issues. If one (or both) of you is not emotionally ready to handle something, you must mutually agree to put it on a backburner until the time is right. There are two exceptions to this: (1) if it involves decisions that are affecting the well-being of children or (2) if they are time-related issues that have urgent deadlines attached to them, such as financial obligations that must be met.

5. Listen with your heart as well as your ears. Male inmates, especially, must keep this in mind. If the visitor is a wife or girlfriend, she does not necessarily want you to fix the problem; she may just want you to understand how she feels. And since you are already feeling frustrated at your inability to fix outside problems, this should actually be a help to you.

6. Identify the real issues, but do so with gentleness and respect. In many cases, the issues expressed are not the real issues; the true sources of conflict may be wrapped up in something else entirely. Sometimes, anger is rooted in unresolved conflicts. For example, family members may be hiding their anger over all the pain and turmoil the incarcerated one has caused because they are afraid to express it. So instead of bringing up the real source of their turmoil, they may verbally attack some smaller failure of either the prisoner or the system.

7. Remember that the conversation should not be dominated by one person. Agree to give one another equal time to talk about what each has been doing. To dominate the discussion is to send the message that only one person's needs are important.

8. Be kind. It's not all about you. I once heard someone say, "Be kind to each other. Everyone is fighting big battles." The shrink-wrapped world of prison life can cause one to become very self-focused. Just as easily, the demands and responsibilities of outside life can cause visitors to become self-focused as well.

9. Make a commitment at the beginning of each visit to make no unreasonable demands on each other. Inmates are often frustrated by their inability to help with pressing needs they see their loved ones going through. Visitors often feel a similar frustration when their loved ones ask for something they cannot do. Make a commitment to each other, early in your journey, that you will both try to be reasonable with your requests, and then stick to it.

10. Ask for practical ways in which you can be of help to each other. The little things are often the most important. Remember, the goal is to build your relationship while apart. By asking your loved one for practical ways that you can express caring and support, you send the message that you have the long haul in view.

Practical Issues to Consider Regarding Visits

Distance from the facility. If the resident is a county inmate, the chances are better that his visitors live fairly close to the facility. But for those serving time in state and federal facilities, it is not uncommon for family members to be separated by hundreds—if not thousands—of miles. For them, visits will be less frequent and more inconvenient. Not only is the expense of travel far greater, but lodging is also a problem. Sometimes family members who come from a great distance plan on visiting several days in a row. This will mean that between visiting times, they will be sitting in a motel room in an unfamiliar part of the country for long, lonely periods of time. How will the time be filled? Transportation will be a challenge. Rent a car? Take a cab? Rely on public transportation? Sometimes, local agencies or churches situated close to the prison provide assistance with the needs of visiting family members. Ask your loved one to look into such possibilities before you arrive. Sometimes, just placing a call to a local church might provide you with leads.

Ann Edenfield[10] provides the reader with several, practical tips for making family preparations to visit your loved one. Her book was the result of having a husband in prison.

Entry procedures. When entering a state or federal institution for the first time, here are some important things to know about typical correctional facility procedures.

1. *Know your loved one's approved visiting schedule.* The many different units within a prison or jail require differing visiting schedules to accommodate everyone. If your loved one has been recently moved to another part of the facility, it is likely his visiting times have also changed. He should notify you if this is the case; however, if he does not, call the institution.

2. *Make sure you are on the approved visitors list.* Most prisons require the residents to submit the names of those they want to visit them. Make sure you are on this list before attempting to visit. Many institutions have a limit to the number of people who can be on a visiting list.

3. *Bring a photo ID.* A driver's license is best, but a passport also works. Some facilities may require your social security number.

4. *Arrive early.* Arrive thirty to forty-five minutes

10. Edenfield, Ann. 2002. *Family Arrested. How to Survive the Incarceration of a Loved One.* Albuquerque, N.M.: Americana Publishing, Inc. The book is now published by Wings Publishing, www.wingsministry.org or 505.291.6412.

early. Processing visitors can take a long time. You will eventually learn what is "normal" for your facility.

5. *Travel light.* Leave whatever items are not needed for the visit in the car. The less you bring in, the quicker you will be processed.

6. *Be aware of the clearance and entry procedures.* Visits are one of the primary ways for contraband items to get into the institution. Be prepared to be searched each and every time you enter the facility. Normally, you will only have to pass through a metal detector or have a hand-wand waved over your body. But many institutions also add routine procedures such as: turning your pockets inside out, opening your mouth for a visual examination, raising your pant legs, taking off your shoes and belts, peeling your socks back or a number of other precautions designed to reveal anything hidden in your clothing or on your person. Inspection officers will also take a thorough look into any items you are bringing in.

7. *Be prepared for the possibility of being strip-searched.* Prison officials are allowed to perform complete body searches any time they wish. Usually conducted in a private room or behind a screen, an officer of the same gender examines the most intimate parts of your body. Many find this procedure humiliating. Children and infants are also subject to such examinations. You can refuse such searches, but your refusal will result in the termination of your visit. These types of searches tend to be random and occasional.

8. *If bringing children, find out what items may be*

brought in to keep them busy in case they get restless.

9. *Bring coins (usually quarters) in case a locker is required to store your belongings.*

10. *Bring additional coins or dollars if the institution has vending machines in the visiting areas.*

11. *Show respect to correctional officers.* Do not enter into an argument with correctional staff, even if you feel they have been insensitive or rude. If you feel you have been offended or treated disrespectfully, report it later to the shift commander. Bear in mind that processing a long line of visitors and inspecting their belongings is a tedious and often unappreciated task. Patience can sometimes wear thin, especially if some of the visitors that went ahead of you were themselves rude or demanding. Your patience and kind words, combined with an attitude of respect, can help to change a negative environment into a positive one.

12. *Never smuggle any illegal substance or item into the facility.* This is a felony offense in most states and you can be prosecuted. It will also result in disciplinary actions against your incarcerated loved one. It can result in additional time being added to his sentence, or the loss of good time.

13. *Observe all rules.* Most facilities will have a posted list of prohibitions concerning visits. Today, most institutions post their departmental information on the Internet. Check the facility's website for the full list. This can include:

- Not wearing provocative clothing
- No excessive jewelry (wedding rings are okay)
- No inappropriate (or unauthorized) physical contact during the visits

- No contraband
- No weapons
- No cash except for approved use of food, drink or candy machines
- Not taking anything out of the institution that you did not bring in

14. *Be prepared for both contact and no-contact visits*. Most state and federal facilities allow contact visits. That is, you and your loved one will be permitted to be in each other's presence without anything separating you physically. However, some county facilities do not permit such visits. If this is your situation, be prepared for the frustration of not being able to touch each other. Your conversation may be conducted over a phone and you will see your loved one through fortified glass or, in some cases, only via a monitor. And while many facilities provide small sound barriers between you and the next visitor, some do not. In such cases, the air is filled with many conversations going on simultaneously; privacy will be minimized and it can be difficult to hear. Remember that all phone conversations during your visit can be monitored and recorded.

15. *Plan ahead for clergy visits*. If you have asked a clergy person to visit your loved one, you should advise him or her to contact the institution before leaving for the visit. Although religious representatives are usually granted special privileges regarding their ability to visit, they are still not allowed to pop in whenever they feel like it. If the institution has a chaplain, call this person first. The chaplain can usually facilitate such visits.

Apart Together

There is another form of communication we have not mentioned. It is what I would call "being together apart." It is a way of sharing life while not actually being together. This is accomplished by doing the same activities at the same times of day. For example, I know couples who study the same Bible passages at the same time each day. Then when they are able to communicate later, they discuss what they have learned. Some read the same book; others write a letter. The important thing is that it is going on at the same time—in real time. You may discover that this form of communication creates a special sense of closeness that is worth the effort.

CHAPTER THREE

Correctional Staff

Just as the jail or prison environment requires an adjustment for your loved one, it makes the same demands upon those who work there. No one is more affected by this than correctional officers (COs) because they are the ones who spend the most time in direct contact with the inmates.

To make a mistake can cost a CO his or her job; and in some severe cases, his or her life. COs must stay in control. In fact, the three "Cs" of the officer's world are "Custody, Care and Control," with the emphasis on the last of these. In an effort to strengthen this aspect of his or her job, COs must maintain an air of professional distance from the inmate population. To be overly friendly can set him or her up for manipulation. As a result, his or her demeanor can appear cold and unfriendly to those who are unfamiliar with the culture. A correctional officer's job requires constant vigilance, control and professionalism.

But always remember that correctional staff are people. Some are friendly and outgoing; others are more reserved. Culturally speaking, it is very difficult for those who do not work in this environment to understand what it is like. Their task should evoke our compassion, not our critique. Society owes them a great debt. These men and women do a very tough job in a very tough environment. But usually, the only times one hears about them is when something goes wrong, or if media portrays them in a negative light. A perspective that might be helpful for you to keep in mind is that they are also protecting your loved one.

Our jail and prison populations continue to expand at a rapid pace. Hundreds of thousands of people are processed through our criminal justice system every year. The stress this places on the entire system cannot help but affect both inmates and staff alike. Treat correctional workers with respect and friendliness. Even if some do not respond the same way, keep it up. Your persistence will have an effect on your relationship with them over the long haul, especially if you see the same officers again and again. If you are consistently respectful, friendly and obedient to the rules, you will notice a marked difference in the way individual officers will treat you after four to six months of visiting.

Are there negative, rude and unfriendly correctional officers? Of course. Are there some who should not be in the positions they are in? Absolutely. However, just as it is true that there are a few bad apples in any bunch, it is equally true that most of these men and women attempt to do their jobs as professionally as possible.

CHAPTER FOUR

Children

One of the saddest things I have witnessed is watching incarcerated moms and dads trying to squeeze out one last minute with their children. I still have a mental image of a little boy at a maximum security prison saying goodbye to his father. His little body was tilting ever sideways as he tried to stay ahead of the sliding steel door that finally separated him from his dad. Prison is a painful experience for everyone involved. To say that it doesn't take a toll on the children would be untrue.

I have known some families who have tried to keep the truth from their younger children. "Daddy is away on a long business trip" mom may say. However, if they are school age, this will usually backfire when someone at school brings it up. I have watched carefree children grow slowly depressed and angry as the months and years go by. School grades of above average students can drop. Behaviors can change; acting out can become more noticeable. Studies have shown that children of incarcerated parents have a significantly higher risk of eventually going to jail themselves. Uncertainty about their future and insecurity about their present affect many little ones who must now face life without a parent.

Working Together

It boils down to this: If you are married and your spouse is now in prison or jail, you are both going to have to put your heads together to come up with a proactive plan for your children. This will not take care of itself. Your challenges are serious, and you need a serious defense. Edenfield has a pointed reminder for parents in this situation: "Remind the incarcerated parent that his duties and his responsibilities to the children have not changed." As helpless as he may now feel, he cannot give up his sense of responsibility. Although he can no longer do as he once did, he must now do what he can.

The task is not impossible. With the right support, your children can experience not only a growing relationship with each of you, but can also emerge as healthy young adults. The first thing you, as parents, must do is to make a promise to each other that you will strengthen your marriage and your relationship. It will mean a concentrated effort to not allow the great hardship of this experience defeat you. Resist the temptation to wallow in the twin swamps of self-pity and self-absorption. This does not mean you pretend that everything is just fine, but it does mean you have an endgame in sight—the health and survival of your family. Put your heads together and continually work on a plan to make the right decisions for your children.

Visiting

Bring the children to see the incarcerated parent. Try to divide the time to allow for interaction with each child but do not sacrifice all your own time.

I once read that the best thing parents can do for their children is to love each other.

If you live close to the jail or prison and can visit frequently, Edenfield recommends you be sensitive to not develop a routine that takes the children away from their own activities every weekend. When her husband was in prison, she didn't want her children to think of their time with dad as a forced obligation; she wanted it to be anticipated out of a true desire to see their father. She also recommends caution regarding the holidays. For these special days, Edenfield didn't want annual trips to

Separation doesn't mean the family bond disappears; it simply means your experience will be different.

a depressing prison to form the backdrop of her children's memories for years to come. She chose to take the kids to see their dad either before or after the event and to celebrate their normal holidays with relatives and friends. While this may not be the choice you wish to make, it does represent the types of things you both need to be thinking about.

Attitude

Believe the best; do not give up. I have friends who have served close to twenty years in prison and later successfully took up with their grown children upon release. Separation doesn't mean the family bond disappears; it simply means your experience will be different. If a long sentence is being served, do not spend the time regretting what is being lost; learn to get the most out of what you have. Your relationship will be experienced differently than others, but if you spend all your time sorrowing over what you cannot have, you will be missing what you do have. If a thriving relationship is your goal, you must determine how to make the most of your own unique situation.

This journey isn't easy. Life without the physical presence of your loved one is extremely difficult. However, if your mutual goals are to grow in your relationship and help your children adjust to this new situation as best as they can, you cannot permit a negative outlook to dominate your thinking. Don't go it alone; find people who will walk with you and support you in a positive way. The person on the inside has to make the same decision. He must be selective about his choice of friends. The prison culture is a tough one; it is easy to get swept up in the negativity and jive, but it is important for him to find a group of fellow inmates who are committed to personal growth and a positive lifestyle.

The Family and Corrections Network offers a list of benefits to children who visit a parent in prison, common questions children ask their incarcerated parent and a developmental guide for preparing children for prison visits. Visit www.fcnetwork.org and click on *Children of Prisoners Library* for more information.

CHAPTER FIVE

The Most Important Relationship of All

Up to this point we have spoken to you about realities that affect your new situation: your loved one in prison and you at home. We have attempted to provide suggestions and to offer insights that can help you during your separation and, at the same time, be relevant to the correctional culture. Our prayer is that these recommendations have been helpful to you.

We also believe that the God of heaven wants to use this experience to draw you into a closer relationship with himself. If you are beginning to feel this might be the case, we encourage you to read these last few pages.

There is a glue in the universe that holds everything together; the Bible says this glue is Jesus Christ.[11] And if Jesus is able to hold the entire universe together with just his word, then he is certainly able to hold you and your loved one together. Jesus, as God the Son, is the glue of all relationships. The key is to be in a right relationship with *him*.

So how does one have a right relationship with God? Believe it or not, it begins with sorrow. Listen

11. Hebrews 1:1-3

to King Solomon, the wisest man who ever lived:

> It is better to go to a house of mourning than to go to a house of feasting, for death is the destiny of every man; the living should take this to heart. Sorrow is better than laughter, because a sad face is good for the heart. The heart of the wise is in the house of mourning, but the heart of fools is in the house of pleasure.[12]

How these words fly in the face of our pleasure-seeking culture! What that paragraph seems to be saying is that it is actually better for us to be at a *funeral* than to be at a *party*. How can this be, you ask? The answer is because we don't get to live forever. All of us are going to die, and if there is something that takes place *after* death, then we need to think about it *before* we die. This is especially true if what we decide in this life determines where we will be in the next.

Over the years, I have had many friends tell me that if they had not come to prison, they would not have gotten serious about God. Prison is a true "house of mourning." I stated at the beginning of this booklet that going to prison is like being buried alive. So here we are, at a funeral parlor—a place of sorrow. And God actually says it is better for us to be here than at a party on the outside.

Jesus said a similar thing: "Happy are those who mourn, for they will be comforted." Isn't comfort what we need right now? Don't our souls cry out for it? Jesus said, "Come to me all you who are weary and burdened, and I will give you rest. Take

---

12. Ecclesiastes 7:2-4

my yoke upon you and learn from me, for I am gentle and humble in heart, and you will find rest for your souls."[13]

The kind of sorrow the Bible is talking about is the deep sadness we feel about our sins. Just as it is right to feel a deep sadness over being separated from our loved one in prison, so the Bible says we should feel a deep sadness over our separation from God. Our sinful choices have caused that separation.[14] Repentance is simply changing our minds about living our own way and desiring in

God sent his only Son to die on a cross as the payment for our sins. It is the *only* payment he will accept.

our hearts to turn to God's way. It means desiring to close the gap between ourselves and God.

So how do we bridge that gap? The pain of our separation and the longing to be forgiven should cause us to reach out for the answer. This is why the sorrow we are experiencing can be called "good." This is why our awful experience has a "better" side to it. If this great tragedy has caused us to seek God, then it has played a most important role in your life.

God sent his only Son to die on a cross as the payment for our sins. It is the *only* payment he will accept. When Jesus died upon that cross in Jerusa-

13. Matthew 11:8, 29
14. Isaiah 59:2

lem two thousand years ago, the precious blood that flowed from his body was the full and total payment for everything you or I have ever done wrong. And once he died and the debt was paid, he rose victoriously from the dead three days later. Only God can do that!

There is no sin so great that Jesus' death on the cross cannot cover it in full. You or your loved one have not done *anything* God is not willing to forgive. The Bible describes everyone in the world as being held in a great prison of sin.[15] In that sense, we have *all* been prisoners. The good news is that he visited us while we were still in prison! Do not let the pain of this awful experience be wasted. If you are truly sorry for the distance between you and God, and want to know that you are truly forgiven, then take him at his word. He said if you would put your trust in Jesus Christ, he would forgive your sins.[16] Now *there* is true comfort!

God said that if we admit with our mouths that "Jesus is Lord," and believe in our hearts that God has raised him from the dead, we will be saved.[17] If you are ready to place your faith in Jesus Christ, then let this little prayer be the cry of your heart:

Dear Father God, I am truly sorry for the sins I have committed. I am sorry that I have been so far away from you. I need you, Oh God. I believe in my heart that Jesus Christ is your Son, and that you sent him to die on the cross for my sins. And I believe that he shed his blood,

---

15. Galatians 3:22
16. John 3:16
17. Romans 10:9-11

died, and rose up from the dead three days later. I want to receive that wonderful gift of your forgiveness and I place my trust in Jesus Christ. Thank you for hearing my prayer, in the name of Jesus. Amen.

If you have a friend whom you know to be a genuine Christian, I encourage you to call him or her immediately. Ask to go to church with him or her, or, if it is too far away, ask the person to help you identify a good church near where you live. It is important for you to grow in your faith and to be around people who have experienced that same wonderful forgiveness.

Pray that your loved one in prison will experience the same thing. Every jail and prison I know has a group of Christian inmates who are faithfully attempting to grow in their faith. Your loved one would do well to be around them. Encourage him to attend the Bible studies and Christian services held there. If there is a chaplain, call and ask him or her to follow up with your loved one. And both of you should begin to read your Bibles daily. It offers a whole new way of living.

May both you and your loved one experience his grace and his peace. It is available only through that most important relationship of all: becoming God's son or daughter through faith in Jesus Christ. May he richly bless you as you begin this journey together.